Get Into The Power

The Top 15 Reasons Why You N___ __ ___ ___ ___
Power (and Profits) of Podcasting

Podcasting is one of the fastest growing industries in the world. Now you can discover how to take advantage of this explosive growth by creating your very own Podcast and tap into multiple streams of income, all while having a blast doing it!

In this revolutionary Itty Bitty Book, best-selling author and veteran Podcast and Radio Coach Christine Blosdale shows you how to use Podcasting to not only promote your own brand and business, but how to profit from it as well.

In this Itty Bitty Podcast Book you will find:

- Expert advice and strategies on how to catapult you forward to become a successful Podcaster.

- What multiple revenue streams are available to you once you start Podcasting.

- Resources and motivation to help you get started.

Pick up a copy of this informative book today and discover the power and profits that come when you dive into the wonderful world of Podcasting.

Your Amazing Itty Bitty® Podcast Book

The Top 15 Reasons Why You Need To Tap Into the Power (and Profits) of Podcasting

Christine Blosdale

Published by Itty Bitty® Publishing
A subsidiary of S & P Productions, Inc.

Printed in the United States of America

Itty Bitty Publishing
311 Main Street, Suite D
El Segundo, CA 90245
(310) 640-8885

ISBN: 978-1-950326-46-4

This book is dedicated to my mother, who told me I could achieve anything in life - and to all of the future Podcasters who become inspired after reading this book.

This is also dedicated to my beautiful wife, Tracy, and our children Millen and Iesha. You are my inspiration in all that I do.

Stop by our Itty Bitty® website Directory to find more interesting information about Podcasting.

Or visit Christine Blosdale at:

ChristineBlosdale.com

Table of Contents

Introduction

So, you're considering jumping into the Wonderful World of Podcasting. Congratulations and welcome!

With an estimated 800,000+ active podcasts in over 100 different languages Podcasting is one of the fastest growing information and entertainment platforms in the world. And the best news is it's growing every single day!

Are you a passionate vegan? A single mom who can feed her family for under $20 a day? Maybe you're a fierce advocate for people with disabilities or the LGBTQ community.

With over 60 million people listening to podcasts each week, no matter where your passion lies or what you're an expert in, chances are there is an audience out there that is hungry for your Podcast show.

In other words, millions of people all around the world are actively looking for new Podcasts that reflect their interests, and one of those could be yours!

Reason #1
Podcasting Is The New Gold Rush and Now Is The Time To Get In!

In addition to the staggering statistics mentioned in the introduction, it is estimated that Podcast ad revenue will reach $1 Billion by 2021.

Now that's some serious money! Wouldn't you like to tap into that?

1. With hundreds of different Podcast genres, Business, Sports, Psychology, Finance, True Crime, Comedy, Spirituality, Relationships, etc., your options are endless on what type of audience you can tap into.
2. Your potential audience is huge! With 51% of the US population having listened to a podcast, when you consider the amount of global listeners, your potential audience increases to hundreds of millions of people.
3. Listeners are more likely to be college educated and more apt to buy from companies or brands mentioned in their favorite podcasts.
4. Podcasts may be popular now, but get ready, it's going to get even bigger!

The Popularity of Podcasts Keeps Growing

Some of Hollywood's biggest stars understand just how powerful Podcasting is. Below are just a few of the big names taking the Podcast plunge.

- Here's The Thing with Alec Baldwin
- Oprah's SuperSoul Conversations
- Will Ferrell's Ron Burgundy Podcast
- Under The Skin with Russell Brand
- RuPaul: What's the Tee?

Major brands like Spotify are claiming that Podcasts will be as important to the company as streaming is for Netflix. Here's why:

- Podcast audiences who subscribe to shows are loyal and devoted fans.
- Many listeners take action in response to hearing an ad during a favorite podcast.
- The average listener spends over 6 hours per week listening to programs.
- Podcasts supply golden marketing opportunities to businesses at an affordable price.
- More people are drastically reducing time in front of a TV and opting for programming that they personally choose.

Reason # 2
Use Podcasting To Promote Your Own Business Or Expand Your Brand

Podcasting can certainly enhance any business or brand by bringing knowledge of what you do to the attention of potentially millions of listeners. I often tell my coaching clients that "there is always an audience for what you have to offer."

If you're a real estate agent, a coach or consultant, a healer, speaker, make-up artist or computer wizard, literally any profession or industry can have a spotlight in the world of Podcasting.

1. Incorporate what you do into the title of your podcast show. For example; "Real Estate Tips with Suzy Seller", pretty much tells you what the podcast is all about plus it promotes your name and brand as well.
2. You can also become your very own media "Sponsor", and mention your business website or special offers to listeners during your podcast.
3. At the beginning and end of every podcast tell people how they can get in touch with you for more information or to book a consultation or session with you.

More Suggestions On How To Promote Your Business On Your Own Podcast

When done right, and with some clever placement on your own show, you can maximize your earning potential by engaging your audience.

- Offer a free bonus E-Book or video program to anyone who signs up for your Podcast Newsletter. Then send out weekly emails about your show and business offerings.
- In the notes or description of your podcast, or in individual episodes, include links to your website, social media and YouTube channel as well as your email address.
- Invite a guest on your show that has a similar business model as yours and talk about the similarities and differences between the two.
- Offer a free 15 or 30 minute consultation or coaching session via Skype or Zoom to anyone who hears of the offer on your podcast. They could be your next paying client!

Reason #3
Promote You (And Your Business) As A Guest On Other Podcasts

Now is the time to step out of the box. Since my personal podcast is called "Out of The Box With Christine", I feel right at home with this one. If you thought promoting your business was all about just having your OWN podcast; think again.

There are literally hundreds of thousands of podcast hosts that are looking for interesting guests to be on their show right now. Why not let that person be you? If you take just a little time to connect with other podcasters, it will definitely pay off.

1. Seek out the shows that would be of benefit for you to be a guest on. For example, if you are, a Medical Intuitive, you may want to look for shows specializing in Health or Healing. If you are a Social Media expert look into podcasts for Entrepreneurs and Business.
2. Once you find podcasts you think you'd be a match for make sure you actually listen to the podcast before asking to be a guest! Nothing turns off a host more than when someone pitches to them when they've never listened to their show.

Get Booked And Get FREE Publicity!

When pitching yourself to be on someone else's podcast make sure you mention the many ways you can benefit them, and why they need you on their show.

- Promise to promote the podcast episode you're featured in, and then really do it!
- Invite the host to be on your show as well and get double exposure from their fan base.
- Offer listeners a free gift or bonus where they need to go to your website, or email you, to gain access.
- Always require that links to your own show and website be listed in the program notes on any podcasts in which you make guest appearances.

Interested in other ways to get booked? You can use guest booking resources like these listed below:

- https://podcastguests.com/
- https://perfectpodcastguest.com
- https://www.radioguestlist.com/

Reason #4
Become An "Expert" Through Your Podcast And Land Speaking Gigs

Podcasters are becoming the new Rockstars of the modern world and with thousands of new fans tuning in every day it is easy to see why. Since launching my very own podcast I have been asked to speak at several large media events, marketing bootcamps and industry seminars, and you can too!

1. Make sure you mention on your show and website that you're available for speaking gigs.
2. On your website list the different areas of expertise you can speak on. Are you an expert at marketing or publicity? Can you turn a tragedy into a positive life lesson? If so, then let people know!
3. The more you speak in public the more people will get to know you and your podcast.

There are opportunities to speak no matter what your niche is. Search for events near you and contact the producer or event coordinator directly. Eventbrite and 10Times.com are wonderful resources for finding out about global events, conferences and expos.

Speaking In Public Is A Confidence Booster And Promotes YOU!

Public speaking is one of the best things you can do as a Podcaster. It helps you gain confidence and creates your authentic "voice". Plus it can lead to opportunities you never knew existed.

Some speaking gigs are paid, some are not, but don't let that deter you. There are wonderful opportunities that await you in public speaking. Here are just a few;

- Take advantage of any and all speaking opportunities. If you need to build up confidence check out Toastmasters International - a non-profit organization that teaches public speaking and leadership skills through a worldwide network of clubs.
- Most events need publicity and promotion. Tell the organizers you'll promote the event on your show and on social media. That shows them you are invested in the success of the event.
- Once you land a gig send a headshot along with links to your show and website so they can promote you.
- If it's not a paid job you may be able to pitch from the stage an offer of some sort. Just find out the specifics prior to saying "yes" and signing on.

Reason #5
Meet Celebrities, Authors,
Movers And Shakers

If you're at all concerned about finding guests for your podcast – don't be! You'd be surprised at who would love to be featured and promoted on your show. Especially if they have something they want to promote like a book, movie or special event.

Over the years I've interviewed thousands of fascinating people like Roseanne Barr, Ed Asner, Marianne Williamson, Wanda Sykes, Kelly Carlin and Ralph Nader just to name a few. With a podcast the possibilities to land great guests are endless.

1. Got a favorite book or TV show? Why not reach out to the publisher or publicity department to ask for an interview? You never know until you ask.
2. Contact major publishing houses and ask to be put on their media and press list.
3. Some celebrities are open to requests made directly online or on social media. Just be professional and ask them if they'd like to be on your show to promote something near and dear to their heart like a charity or organization.

Hurray For Hollywood - No Matter Where You Are From

You don't need to have a famous person or celebrity on your podcast to boost listenership, but it sure does help when you have someone people have heard of before, and perhaps even admire. And why not seize the opportunity to help bring new listeners to your show?

- Try booking a writer you love by contacting their publisher's publicity department. Hint; search the author's latest book title on Amazon and scroll down to the listed Publishing house. That's who you need to contact.
- Follow the social media accounts of celebrities you admire and direct message them a query with a link to your very best podcast show.
- Do a search on http://www.PRWeb.com with the keywords; book signing, celebrity, movie, premiere, actor or athlete. Then contact the person listed in the press release as the Media Contact.

Some additional resources for famous guests and show ideas:
- https://www.helpareporter.com/
- https://journalistsresource.org/
- https://www.imdb.com/

Reason #6
Share Your Passions and Inspire Others

For the first time in human history, you now have the ability to tap into millions of people who share the same passions as you. And if you use your podcast in the best way possible you might even be able to inspire a few as well along the way.

1. If you have a passion for helping others why not talk about it? Inform people on how they can assist the elderly or perhaps volunteer at a dog rescue center. It creates a feels-good-to-do-good kind of energy and just think about the lives you can impact!
2. Ever have a turning point in life like surviving cancer or losing a lot of weight because your life depended upon it? Why not share your story and help inspire others?
3. Whatever you are passionate about in life there is an audience. Do you love to garden? Collecting sports memorabilia? Tinkering on vintage cars? Whatever you love to do as a hobby can become the foundation of a wonderful podcast show.

Your Passions Can Connect You To The Public

Below are just a few of the passion fueled podcast genres you can jump into:

- Netflix Addicts Unite
- In Our Seventies and Still Sexy
- Gluten Free and Loving It
- Parents and Families of Autistic Children
- Cleaning and Organization Shortcuts
- Tinkering With Tech Geeks
- True Crime Book of The Week
- Veterans Helping Veterans

An added bonus of passion driven podcasting is being able to inspire others. With my own show, Out of The Box With Christine, I've had listeners tell me that they've gained the courage to leave an abusive relationship, lose a few pounds and even start that book they've always wanted to write.

Don't Forget

1. Be authentic and come from your heart because people will feel it.
2. You never know who you will inspire!

Reason #7
Use Your Podcast To Help Others

One of the most powerful and rewarding aspects of having your own podcast show is the ability to advocate for issues that are important to you.

Bringing attention to people or organizations that are doing good in the world is a wonderful use of your podcast, and your audience will appreciate you for it.

Whether it be a food sharing program or social services for those in need, the list of important philanthropic organizations that you could showcase is endless.

1. Talk about government programs and services that help people with disabilities. https://www.usa.gov/disability-programs
2. Advocate for people to get involved with animal welfare (no kill) organizations. https://bestfriends.org/
3. Help children and teens in foster care get safe, loving and permanent families. https://www.adoptuskids.org/
4. Have a guest talk about the right to clean air, clean water, and healthy communities. https://www.nrdc.org/

13

The More We Know The More We Can Help

Imagine if you used your weekly podcast to spotlight a group of people doing wonderful things for their communities. In 52 weeks you could shine a bright light on 52 important resources that your listeners should know about.

- Feeding America is a nationwide network of more than 200 food banks and food rescue organizations.
  https://www.feedingamerica.org
- Doctors Without Borders provides medical services in war-torn regions.
  https://www.doctorswithoutborders.org/
- Habitat For Humanity helps families build and improve places to call home.
  https://habitat.org/
- Do Something is a global not-for-profit exclusively for young people and social change.
  https://www.dosomething.org/us

Want more ideas on how to use your podcast to help others?

- Do a search using keywords "non-profit" or "charities" and contact those in charge of press or media at organizations that resonate with you.

Reason # 8
Show Me The Money! Tapping Into Multiple Streams of Income

For many of you, this is the chapter you've been waiting for. Or maybe you jumped directly to this page because you want to know exactly how much money you can make with your podcast.

As with any business, it really depends on how much effort you're willing to put into it. But with millions of potential listeners and numerous multiple streams of possible income, podcasting offers a variety of ways to show you the money!

1. Advertising and Sponsorships – If you have a large audience there are podcast ad networks (like Midroll, AdvertiseCast and Archer Avenue) that will connect you with advertisers.
2. If you're just starting out you can directly contact businesses that would be a great fit for your audience and ask them to sponsor you.

More Ways To Generate Income

- Ask for donations to help pay for production costs via membership platforms like Patreon or PayPal.
- If there's a product or service you love you might be able to promote an affiliate offer. Check out <u>Amazon</u>, <u>CJ Affiliate</u> and <u>Share A Sale</u> if you want to tap into affiliate marketing.
- Use programs like <u>Zoom</u> to create your own webinars or workshops that you promote during your show and charge a registration fee for participants.
- Sell your E-books or services (like coaching or consulting) thru your podcast's website.
- Become a public speaker and either charge for your appearance or make a pitch at the end of your presentation to gain new clients or customers.
- Sell merchandise to your fans who would love a t-shirt or baseball cap. It's also great advertising! <u>Printful</u> makes it easy to create hundreds of products and ships them out for you as well.
- Create "premium" content not available to the public, but only to those with a paid membership (check out <u>Kartra</u>) or a pay-per-view type of program like <u>Vimeo</u>.

Reason #9
Market Yourself As A Leader In Your Industry

We have already established that podcasting is a huge hit with a lot of people. And according to the research, the average podcast listener is someone that you definitely want to impress.

MusicOomph has reported that the average podcast consumer is male, under 44, and is 56 percent more likely to be college educated. He is also more likely to have an income over $75,000 and 45 percent more likely to earn over $250,000.

Those numbers are significant because if you can market yourself to this demographic, you'll not only have an affluent audience more apt to follow you (and more likely to buy what you're selling), but you'll also be seen as an expert in your industry. And that can lead to other amazing opportunities.

1. Go beyond your Podcast by being a guest on other shows.
2. Land speaking opportunities at local venues and let listeners know so they can come meet you. And record it all for future use!
3. Create a companion YouTube channel.

Ways To Market Yourself As A Leader

How can you create that spark that sets you apart from the crowd?

- Showcase and share your expertise and knowledge. If you're an expert in a chosen field freely share some tidbits of wisdom with your audience, and often.
- Be responsible for building a community or sparking a movement. Being of service to others or helping solve a problem is key to gaining momentum.
- Create an affiliate program for people to start promoting you and your expertise. When an affiliate makes a sale for you they get paid and you get a virtual marketing team spreading the word about your services and/or products. Programs like iDevAffiliate and 1ShoppingCart make it easy to get started!
- Create new social media groups around your podcast genre and spark dialogue with those who join.
- Become a Sponsor of other Podcast shows that target your audience and market yourself as a leader in your field of expertise. It's affordable and great marketing!

Reason #10
Because It's FUN!

If you are considering creating your own Podcast or being a guest on someone else's – one thing can be said for both – they're a whole lot of fun!

Yes, there can be major work involved too. However, once you see the fun in the creative freedom, I think you'll agree it is worth it.

Hosting your own Podcast allows you the freedom to:

1. Talk about your favorite subjects - plus you get to meet new and exciting people.
2. Bring attention to a cause that is near and dear to your heart.
3. Explore multiple streams of income like donations, affiliates, merchandising, exclusive content, paid ads and more!

Being a guest on a Podcast allows you the freedom to:

1. Promote your own business, product or service to a worldwide audience.
2. Enjoy a conversation that is centered around what excites and motivates you.

How Fun? Let Us Count The Ways

Podcasting can provide endless amounts of enjoyment and satisfaction.

- Getting rave reviews from listeners and fans is always fun. Always!
- The journey of learning something new, like the technical aspects of podcasting, can be rewarding in many ways.
- If you want to guarantee lots of fun, consider booking a comedian as a guest so you and your listeners can laugh thru the entire show.
- Friendship is Fun! You'd be amazed at how many of your guests will become new (and lasting) friends.

Once you have your podcast up and running, why not share the fun with others?

- Create short humorous clips from your show (with apps like VlogEasy) and share on social media. You will be sharing the joy while marketing your podcast.
- If you are going to be a speaker at an event or seminar share that news with your audience and celebrate on air!

Reason #11
Embrace Your Inner Techno Geek

One of the coolest aspects of Podcasting is all of the amazing gadgets and gizmos that can make you sound like a million bucks and expand your reach.

While you don't need to break the bank to sound like a pro, you will need to make an investment for equipment if you want to make an impact.

The basics are; a good computer with Wi-Fi, headphones and a rock solid microphone. You will also need a quality Podcast hosting service like Libsyn or Podbean and sound editing software like GarageBand (for Mac), Pro Tools or my personal fave, Adobe Audition.

Since a quality mic is really the most important tool you will use, here are some recommendations that you might consider..

1. Blue Yeti Condenser USB Mic
2. Audio-Technica AT2020 USB Mic
3. Rode NT-USB Mic
4. Shure SM7B Cardioid XLR Mic
5. Rode NT1-A Vocal XLR Mic

More Gadgets And Tools Of The Trade

Want to fully tap into your inner Techno Geek?
Consider these optional add-ons to your home
based Podcast Studio.

1. Rode RODECaster Pro Podcast
   Production Studio
2. Yamaha MG-10 10 Input Stereo Mixer
3. iRig Lavalier Mic
4. Collapsible Chroma Key Green Screen
   (perfect for video podcasts and webinars)
5. Adjustable Portable Sound Absorbing
   Vocal Recording Panel
6. Seagate Backup Plus 5TB external
   portable hardrive – a must-have to
   organize and store audio and video files
   (which can be quite large in size) of all of
   your shows.

Stay up-to-date on all of the latest recommended
products and technology for Podcasters by
visiting these resources..

- Podcraft: Honing The Art of Podcasting
- PodcastMagazine.com
- ThePodcastHost.com

Reason #12
Gain Confidence And Influence Others

As with many new endeavors in life, in the very beginning it can seem intimidating simply because it is something you haven't done before.

Remember the first time you rode a bike without training wheels? You may have felt like you were going to crash into something. But once you mastered your balance you were able to ride that bike with confidence and you gained a feeling of freedom.

Podcasting is a lot like riding that bike. With this powerful platform it can take you to places you never dreamed of. With each new show you create (and new fan you gain) your confidence will be boosted and your influence will begin to spread around the globe.

1. Remember to take your time and create a few "test" shows in the beginning. Don't worry if it is not perfect - you'll be a pro in no time!
2. Your podcast can inspire people to start a new path in life or motivate them to make a positive change. The choice is yours.

More Tips To Keep In Mind

Gaining confidence and influencing others comes easier when you are doing something you truly love so make sure your shows are focused on subjects you are passionate about.

If you feel you need more help in the confidence department consider these helpful tips;

- Practice listening to your own voice. This may seem like a no brainer, but you'd be surprised at how many people don't like the sound of their own voice. This is something you must get over if you want to be a successful podcaster. I coach my clients to sing in the shower or in the car to begin to love hearing their own voice.
- Remember to not be too hard on yourself. Listen to your first shows with a kind heart. Everyone is a beginner at something in life. Soon you will feel confident in your ability to communicate.
- Practice interviewing those close to you (maybe family and friends who won't judge you harshly) and ask for positive constructive feedback.

Reason #13
Build Community Or Build An Empire

With your newfound super power of Podcasting you now have the ability to build up a community of like-minded people who share your passion for a cause – or you can begin to build your empire on a whole host of business opportunities.

1. Building Community – Consider joining forces with other podcasters or organizations with the same mission in life. Perhaps you can network and share resources or support each other in some meaningful ways. Start a Facebook Group or hold monthly networking events either online or in person at various venues in large cities. People are the real power behind communities so don't be afraid to get out there and mingle!

2. Building an Empire – Use as many of the tools available to you as you can when expanding the reach beyond your podcast. Create a companion website, market yourself as an expert speaker, coach or consultant. Get paid for your experience and knowledge!

Some Helpful Tips To Get You Started

Building Community is about getting people involved.

- Start a "feel good experience project" that listeners can get involved in. Challenge them to make Care Bags for the Homeless or donate time at a local animal shelter. Recognizing people is great for building community so make sure to thank them!
- Host regular (weekly or monthly) live Facebook chats and ask friends and family to help spread the word.

Building an Empire can take time, but with a podcast you have a global audience to help you.

- Have plenty of purchasing opportunities embedded in your website such as consulting, books, merchandise, etc.
- Did you know you can make money on YouTube? Some people are making six figure incomes! Post your shows as videos and build up your followers on YouTube by promoting it on your podcast and vice versa.
- Maximize the monetization of your podcast by creating your very own MasterMind Group and charge people accordingly based on your expertise and one-on-one time.

Reason #14
The Possibilities Are Endless

Once you begin your Podcast adventure the possible opportunities are really astounding. Here are just a few..

1. Create additional Podcasts in different genres or niches to reach more people.
2. Trade out guest spots with your favorite Podcasters to gain new followers.
3. Create blogs from your show transcripts to maximize search engine results. Temi.com is great for audio-to-text transcriptions.
4. Become an inspirational speaker at local events to talk about your Podcast journey.
5. Ask Local TV and Radio stations to feature you as a guest on their shows.
6. Produce events with fellow Podcasters to expand your influence - and get paid!
7. Transcribe a series of episodes and make a book or E-book out of it – ie; "20 Women CEOs Who Broke Thru The Glass Ceiling."
8. Other Podcasters may want to share resources and ideas with you. Join forces with those who are already successful.

Examples Of What You Can Achieve

The power of Podcasting is so hot right now even former US President Barack Obama and his wife Michelle have become Podcasters.

But you don't need to be a former head of state to benefit from Podcasting. Since I've started my own journey I've been given many opportunities:

- Became a #1 International Amazon best-selling author.
- Named as an Icon of Influence and became a Featured Speaker at numerous Expos, Seminars and Bootcamps.
- I also have the most amazing clients that I coach and consult with on a daily basis.

The things you can do once you have your own Podcast show are truly amazing. But it's really all up to you and how much energy you put into it.

As with so many other aspects of life, you need to take action in order to make things happen. You need to step into this opportunity with passion and with purpose!

Are you excited yet? You should be. Are you ready? Then turn to the next page.

Reason #15
The Time is Now. So What Are You Waiting For?

In this Itty Bitty Book you have been given just a few of the top reasons why you should jump into the magical and marvelous world of Podcasting.

With the popularity of Podcasting continuing to grow and evolve the opportunities for storytellers and brand creators are growing as well.

So, are you ready to get started? Are you ready to get on that mic and shine? Here are a few things you may want to consider doing right away.

1. Do some research before nailing down the name of your Podcast. Make sure it isn't already taken and once you've made a decision make sure you trademark it!
2. Secure a domain for your companion website at Google Domains and check out website hosting services like Squarespace, Wordpress or Wix.
3. Network with others by attending Podcast conferences and seminars to expand your knowledge and skills.
4. Find yourself a mentor or coach who can help guide you thru the process of creating and marketing your Podcast.

Working With A Mentor or Coach

If you are excited about getting started but, are still feeling a bit overwhelmed by it all, don't fret, you are in great company! Lots of people starting out feel the same way you do.

Luckily there is a solution for any anxiety you may be experiencing, and that is to get yourself a qualified mentor or coach. Find someone who can offer their expertise to help you save money, time and frustration.

It doesn't matter if you want to produce your own Podcast or if you just want to be a guest on shows to promote your business or brand, having your own mentor or coach is a great way to get started!

I would love the opportunity to assist you on this incredible journey and if you'd like to schedule a Strategy Session just email me at OutOfTheBoxWithChristine@gmail.com. You can also visit ChristineBlosdale.com to find Reviews and Testimonials from people I have worked with.

Need ideas for your own Podcast? Subscribe to my show at OutOfTheBoxWithChristine.com or access all of my episodes on YouTube at bit.ly/outoftheboxyoutube

You've finished. Before you go…

Tweet/share that you finished this book.

Please star rate this book.

Reviews are solid gold to writers. Please take a few minutes to give us some itty bitty feedback on this book.

ABOUT THE AUTHOR

Christine Blosdale is an Amazon #1 Best Selling Author, Podcast Host and Coach, On-Air Radio Personality, Public Speaker and a Multi-Million Dollar Fundraiser.

She is the host of Out of The Box With Christine - the popular podcast for socially conscious entrepreneurs - and has over 18 years experience in broadcast journalism.

Christine has produced The Roseanne Barr Radio Show and has interviewed such notables as Marianne Williamson, Ralph Nader, Kelly Carlin, Ed Asner, Dr. Judith Orloff, and Nobel Peace Prize laureate Wangari Maathai.

Capitalizing off her innate ability to know what draws in and captivates an audience, Christine has also gained exposure for hundreds of entertainers, authors and entrepreneurs to get their brand and business out into the world.

An all-in-one passionate public speaker, podcast and radio coach and major force for manifesting good in the world, Christine has a solid reputation in the industry based on decades of experience.

For more information visit ChristineBlosdale.com

If you enjoyed this Itty Bitty® book you might also like…

- **Your Amazing Itty Bitty® Advanced Video Marketing Book** – Gary Howard

- **Your Amazing Itty Bitty® Prospect to Profit Book** – Erin Smilkstein

- **Your Amazing Itty Bitty® How to Become a Keynote Speaker** – Lisa Haisha

Or any of the many Amazing Itty Bitty® books available on line at www.ittybittypublishing.com